EDUCATION LIBRARY SERVICE

Browning Way
Woodford Park Industrial Estate
Winsford
Cheshire CW7 2JN

Phone: 01606 592551/557126
Fax: 01606 861412
www.cheshire.gov.uk/els/home.htm

CHESHIRE
COUNTY COUNCIL

Our World

Oceans

By Katie Harker

Aladdin/Watts
London • Sydney

© Aladdin Books Ltd 2006

Designed and produced by
Aladdin Books Ltd
2/3 Fitzroy Mews
London W1T 6DF

**First published in
Great Britain in 2006 by**
Franklin Watts
96 Leonard Street
London EC2A 4XD

A catalogue record for this
book is available from the
British Library.

ISBN 0 7496 6262 X

Printed in Malaysia

Editor:
Harriet Brown

Designers:
Flick, Book Design and Graphics
Simon Morse

Picture researcher:
Alexa Brown

Literacy consultant:
Jackie Holderness – former Senior
Lecturer in Primary Education,
Westminster Institute,
Oxford Brookes University

Photocredits:
Abbreviations: l-left, r-right, b-bottom, t-top,
c-centre, m-middle
Front cover – Stockbyte. Back cover – Comstock.
1, 2-3, 9ml, 26tl, 30tr – Comstock, 3bl, 4ml, 6tl,
8tl, 8bl, 13br, 14tl, 15tl, 17t, 17bl, 18tl, 20tr, 22tl,
25tr – Corbis, 9tl, 16tr, 16bl, 29tr – Corel, 24bl,
30mr – Digital Vision, 27tl – NOAA / Antonio
Pais, 19tl – NOAA / Bill Keogh, 4bl, 14bl – NOAA
/ Matt Wilson and Jay Clark, 13mr - NASA's
Earth Observatory, 11tl, 30br - OAR/National
Undersea Research Program (NURP); Univ. of
Connecticut, 3tl, 3mtl, 12bl, 21tr, 26bl, 27br, 29bl
– Photodisc, 9br, 10tl, 10bl, 12tr, 15br, 28tr, 31tl
– Stockbyte, 23tl – www.istockphoto.com / Bob
Ainsworth, 22bl – www.istockphoto.com / Greg
Nicholas, 18bl – www.istockphoto.com / Laura
Wile, 6bl – www.istockphoto.com / Lisa Devlin,
28bl – www.istockphoto.com / Lise Gagne, 21bl –
www.istockphoto.com / Paul Senyszyn, 20bl –
www.istockphoto.com / Radu Razvan, 24tr –
www.istockphoto.com / Simon Edwin, 3mbl, 19br
– www.istockphoto.com / Tim Gasperak

CONTENTS

Notes to parents and teachers

This series has been developed for group use in the classroom as well as for children reading on their own. In particular, its differentiated text allows children of mixed abilities to enjoy reading about the same topic. The larger size text (A, below) offers apprentice readers a simplified text. This simplified text is used in the introduction to each chapter and in the picture captions. This font is part of the © Sassoon family of fonts recommended by the National Literacy Early Years Strategy document for maximum legibility. The smaller size text (B, below) offers a more challenging read for older or more able readers.

Animal life

Scientists think that life on Earth began in the oceans, over two billion years ago.

A

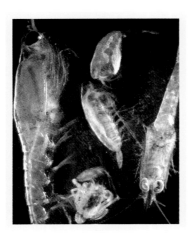

◀ **Without plankton, the ocean's larger animals would die.**

One of the most important food sources for marine life are tiny plants and animals called '**plankton**'.

B

4

Questions, key words and glossary

Each spread ends with a question which parents and teachers can use to discuss and develop further ideas and concepts. Further questions are provided in a quiz on page 30. A reduced version of pages 30 and 31 is shown below. The illustrated 'Key words' section is provided as a revision tool, particularly for apprentice readers, in order to help with spelling, writing and guided reading as part of the literacy hour. The glossary is for more able

or older readers. In addition to the glossary's role as a reference aid, it is also designed to reinforce new vocabulary and provide a tool for further discussion and revision. When glossary terms first appear in the text they are highlighted in bold.

 **See how much you know!**

How much of the Earth is covered in ocean water?

What are the names of the five oceans?

What types of food do we get from the ocean?

How do the oceans affect the weather?

What does overfishing mean?

Where is the 'Mid-Atlantic ridge'?

How do scientists study the ocean floor?

What is causing the sea levels to rise?

Key words
Coral

A

Algae	Continent
Current	Fossil
Mammal	Ocean
Pollution	Seafood
Seagrass	Seaweed
Shellfish	Tide
Wave	Whale

Glossary

Condense – To turn from a gas into a liquid.
Continent – One of the main land masses of the Earth. For example, Africa.
Equator – An imaginary line that runs around the centre of planet Earth.
Evaporate – When a liquid, such as water, turns into a gas.
Friction – When two surfaces rub together they create friction.
Generator – A machine that is used to produce electricity.

B

Gills – A fish's breathing organs.
Global warming – An increase in the temperature on Earth. This may be caused by a build-up of carbon dioxide in the atmosphere.
Plankton – Tiny plants and animals which live in the ocean.

What are oceans?

Ocean water covers around 70 per cent of the Earth's surface. That is about 844 million km². Ocean water is salty. It is full of animals that we eat, and valuable minerals that we use. Oceans are also a useful transport route.

◀ **There is a lot of water on planet Earth.**

Earth is the only planet in the Solar System that has liquid water. If the Earth was much nearer the Sun, the Sun would heat the water and make it **evaporate**. If the Earth was much further from the Sun's heat, it would be very cold and the water would turn into ice.

There are five oceans.

The Pacific, the Atlantic, the Indian, the Southern and the Arctic Ocean are the five oceans. They are connected, but they contain large pieces of land called '**continents**'. There are also many seas. Seas are smaller parts of an ocean that are partly enclosed by land. The largest seas are the South China Sea, the Caribbean Sea and the Mediterranean Sea.

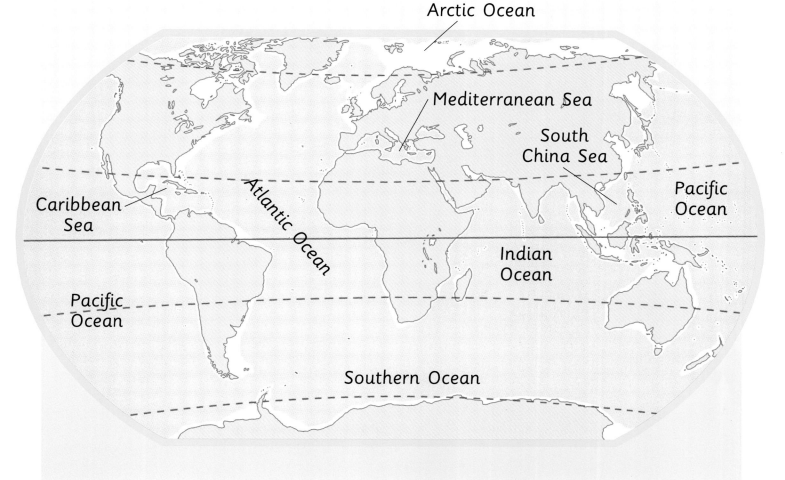

Arctic Ocean

Mediterranean Sea

South China Sea

Pacific Ocean

Caribbean Sea

Atlantic Ocean

Pacific Ocean

Indian Ocean

Southern Ocean

How could a message in a bottle travel around the world?

The water cycle

In hot weather, water from the ocean changes into water vapour. The vapour forms clouds. Some of these clouds drift across the sky and rain down on the land. The rainwater flows into streams and rivers. Then it flows back into the ocean again.

◀ **Near the North and South Poles, the water is less salty.**

The ocean waters near the North and South Poles are full of icebergs. In hot weather the icebergs melt a little and dilute the ocean water so that it becomes less salty. Rain and snow in the polar regions also dilute the ocean water.

◀ The oceans can change colour.

We sometimes talk about the 'deep, blue ocean'. This is because we see it reflecting the blue colour of the sky. However, on a cloudy day the ocean can look grey.

The salt in ocean water comes from the land.

When rainwater flows through rivers, it picks up minerals, like salt, from the soil and rocks on the river-bed. It drops these into the ocean. Ocean water becomes more concentrated with salt as the water evaporates.

 What happens to water that has evaporated from the ocean?

Ocean features

The surface of the Earth has cliffs and valleys. These lumps and bumps are also found on the land under the oceans. It is hard to study the ocean floor because the oceans are very deep. We know very little about the deepest parts of the ocean.

◀ The oceans are less deep near a continent.

The ocean floor slopes up to meet the land so these parts are shallower. Under the Atlantic Ocean there is a huge ridge that is made up of some mountains. The water is less deep near this 'Mid-Atlantic ridge'. The deepest part of the ocean is over 11 kilometres deep. However, most parts of the ocean are about three kilometres deep.

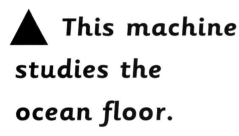

▲ **This machine studies the ocean floor.**

The ocean floor is difficult to study because it is very dark at these depths. The water pressure is also very high. High water pressure can crush underwater machines if they are not strong enough.

The deeper down you are, the darker it is.

Scientists divide the ocean water into three zones of 'light'. These zones are used to describe the areas where marine life can be found.

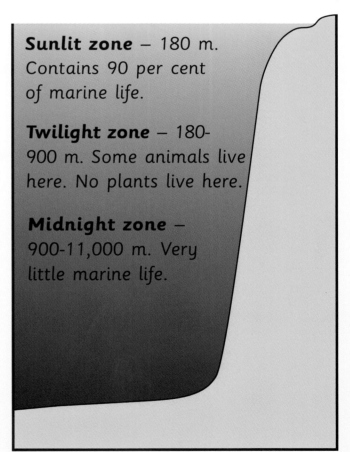

Sunlit zone – 180 m. Contains 90 per cent of marine life.

Twilight zone – 180-900 m. Some animals live here. No plants live here.

Midnight zone – 900-11,000 m. Very little marine life.

 Why isn't the ocean floor a good home for marine life?

Always in motion

Ocean water is always moving. The wind and the pull of the tides cause the ocean water to move. A large mass of moving ocean water is called a 'current'. Currents can be very strong.

◀ **Strong winds make large waves.**

Waves are caused by the wind blowing over the ocean. When wind passes over water there is some **friction**. This pushes the water upwards. Ocean waves can be really big. Big waves can form when strong winds blow over a long stretch of water.

▶ Ocean water moves around in currents.

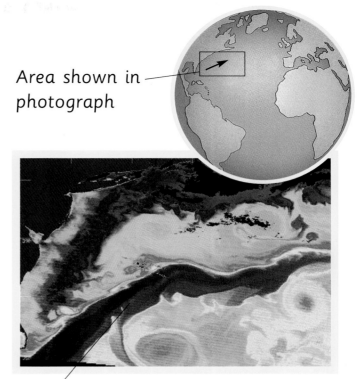

Area shown in photograph

The heat of the Sun warms the oceans nearest to the **Equator**. This warm water current moves towards the North and South Poles. This forces colder water to move towards the Equator. The Gulf Stream is an ocean current.

The Gulf Stream flows across the Atlantic.

The tides are caused by the Moon.

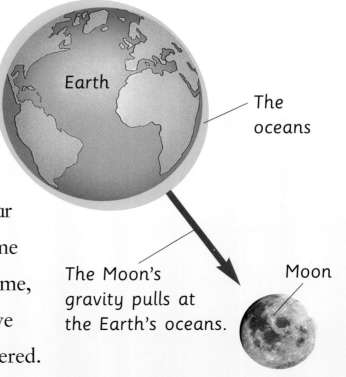

Earth

The oceans

The Moon's gravity pulls on the Earth's ocean water. This causes a 'bulge' of water. The seashores near the bulge have high tide and become covered with water. At the same time, seashores away from the bulge have low tide and the seashore is uncovered.

The Moon's gravity pulls at the Earth's oceans.

Moon

 Why must swimmers be careful where there is a strong current?

Animal life

Scientists think that life on Earth began in the oceans, over two billion years ago. Today, the oceans are full of marine life. Marine life includes any living creature in the oceans. As scientists continue their studies, new ocean creatures are being found all the time.

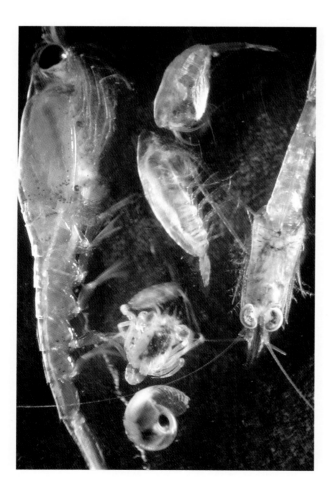

◀ Without plankton like these, the ocean's larger animals would die.

One of the most important food sources for marine life are tiny plants and animals called '**plankton**'. Plant plankton grow using energy from sunlight. Their energy is passed on when animal plankton feed on them. Larger animals get their energy by eating both plant and animal plankton.

◀ Fish can breathe underwater.

Fish, including sharks, don't have lungs like ours. Instead, they breathe with their '**gills**'. The gills take tiny particles of oxygen from the water. A fish can't take oxygen from the air.

Coral reefs are home to many creatures.

Coral reefs are found in warm, shallow waters. They are home to around a quarter of marine life, including algae, fish and snails. Coral is made of tiny animals called 'coral polyps'. When they die, their skeletons form the coral reef.

 Which other marine animals do you know?

Marine mammals

Marine mammals, like whales and dolphins, spend all of their lives in the ocean. A marine mammal is any warm-blooded creature that lives in the ocean, gives birth to its young and feeds them with milk.

◀ **Marine mammals need to breathe air like humans.**

Marine mammals need to breathe oxygen to stay alive. Because they do not have gills, marine mammals swim to the surface to breathe oxygen from the air. Whales and dolphins breathe through a blowhole in the top of their head.

▲ **The blue whale is the largest animal on Earth.**

The blue whale can be over 30 metres long. It weighs the same as 80 elephants and its tongue is the size of a car! Whales grow this big because the ocean water supports their weight. A land animal of this size would not be able to walk.

A seal is a marine mammal.

Marine mammals include seals, whales, dolphins, manatees and sea otters. Marine mammals give birth to their young. Most marine mammals have some hair on their body too.

 What happens to a whale if it gets stranded on a beach?

Plant life

The shallow or sunlit parts of the ocean are full of plant life. There are two main types of marine plants – algae and seagrasses. Plant plankton is one of the simplest types of algae. It is eaten by animal plankton and other animals.

◀ **Seaweed is a type of algae.**

Seaweed is commonly found washed up on the seashore. It can be red, brown or green. Seaweed is a good source of food for many marine animals. Seaweed can also be used to make ice cream, toothpaste, make-up and even clothes!

◀ **This fish is hiding in seagrass.**

Seagrasses have roots that attach to the ocean floor. Seagrass roots absorb nutrients but they do not absorb water like land plants. Small plants and animals live in and on seagrasses.

Ocean plants need sunlight to grow.

Plants are only found in the sunlit zone of the ocean where there is enough light for them to grow. They also thrive here, where the water is warmer. Animals eat ocean plants.

 Why do plants need sunlight to grow well?

Oceans and the weather

Ocean water and currents can affect the weather. The water temperature warms or cools the air. Warm ocean water evaporates to form clouds. Ocean currents also help to move heat around the globe.

◀ **The oceans are warmer in autumn than in summer.**

When the Sun shines on the ocean, the surface warms up. Air can warm up and cool down very quickly but water takes longer to change temperature. By the time the autumn comes, the ocean has been fully warmed by the heat of the summer Sun.

▶ The weather changes less at the seaside than inland.

In the winter, the ocean water heats the air and land nearby. In the summer, the water cools the surrounding air and land. This keeps temperatures at the seaside more constant than inland.

Water in the oceans can evaporate and make a fog.

When strong winds blow over the ocean they cause tiny droplets of spray to fly into the air. If these droplets evaporate in the heat they can leave tiny grains of salt behind. These salt grains encourage the water vapour in the air to **condense** (turn back into water) forming a mist or fog.

 How would temperatures be different if there were no oceans?

Oceans and history

The oceans hold the answers to many important questions about the Earth. The rocks underneath the ocean tell us about the Earth in ancient times. Fossils are the ancient remains of plants and animals. Fossils can be found in the ocean floor.

◀ **Oil rigs help us find oil beneath the ocean.**

Mineral oil comes from the remains of animals and plants that lived millions of years ago. These remains were slowly buried by mud and sand. Over millions of years, heat from the Earth and pressure from the water turned some of these remains into oil and gas. Scientists think there could be a great deal of oil beneath the ocean, still waiting to be discovered.

◀ Many fossils lie deep in the ocean floor.

Fossils found in the ocean floor help us to record the history of life on Earth. Some fossils date back to about 230 million years ago, when dinosaurs were alive.

Some dinosaurs used to live in the oceans.

Mosasaurs were dinosaurs that lived in the oceans millions of years ago. These reptiles grew up to 10 metres long. They ate large fish, turtles and other dinosaurs. They swam by waving their tail from side to side and they used their flippers to steer.

Mososaurus

 Which other dinosaurs can you name?

Using the oceans

The oceans are very useful to us. We take salt from ocean water and building materials from the ocean floor. We catch seafood to eat. We use boats to transport goods. We also make some medicines from marine life such as algae and snails.

◀ **Fish and shellfish are popular seafoods.**

We hunt and catch marine animals for our food. Seafood, such as prawns, cod and tuna, are popular foods. However, some people also eat more unusual creatures like octopus and jellyfish. Many people eat seaweed, and the salt that we add to our food also comes from the oceans.

▶ The ocean is a useful form of transport.

The oceans are used to transport goods, packages and people. Unlike roads, or railways, oceans are a ready-made surface on which to travel. It is cheaper to transport goods across the ocean by ship than by aeroplane.

The oceans can be used to produce electricity.

A power station is used to turn the energy from ocean tides and waves into electricity. Inside this machine (below), the rise and fall of the water forces air to move. The air causes the machinery to turn. As the 'turbine' turns it causes a '**generator**' to move. The generator changes the movement into electricity.

Air movement Electricity

Air chamber

Waves

Turbine

Which fish and seafood do you like to eat?

Looking after the oceans

The oceans are an important natural resource and a beautiful feature of planet Earth. Sadly, many human activities are harmful to marine life. The balance of life in the oceans is under threat. Luckily, some people are trying to look after the oceans.

◀ Global warming is making the sea levels rise.

Pollution in the air may be causing the planet to become warmer. This global warming is melting glaciers and ice caps. This could make ocean levels rise dramatically. If the ocean water rises too much, some towns and cities will disappear as they become completely flooded. Very low countries (such as The Netherlands) are also in danger.

◀ Some fish are dying out because of overfishing.

Parts of the ocean are being 'overfished' as we take more fish from the ocean than can be replaced. Because no one owns the oceans, it is hard to control how many fish are caught. Fishing trawlers can also damage the seabed as they drag their nets along the bottom. Animals like dolphins get caught in the nets and die.

The ocean is becoming very polluted.

In the past, sewage and industrial waste was dumped in the ocean. This harmed marine life so there are now restrictions on ocean waste disposal. Tourism is also a problem. Rubbish in beach resorts is swept into the ocean.

How is marine life harmed by overfishing?

The future

To protect the oceans for the future we need to clean up ocean pollution and look after marine life. The bottom of the oceans is still a mystery. In the future, scientists will learn more about the oceans' secrets.

◀ In the future, the oceans could be a source of drinking water.

As the world population increases we need more clean water to drink. Scientists are looking at ways to remove the salt from seawater so that it is safe to drink. One way to remove the salt is to force the water through a kind of 'sieve' with very small holes.

▶ *We need to work together to protect the oceans.*

The oceans cover most of our planet but no one country takes responsibility for keeping them clean. In the future, governments will need to work together to care for the oceans. They will need to protect and restore coral reefs and rescue endangered marine life.

Power stations may use metal from the ocean.

Deuterium is a metal that is found dissolved in water. Scientists want to use this metal in nuclear power stations to produce electricity. If scientists can use this nuclear power safely, we may have a new source of energy that would last for millions of years.

? Why do we need to protect the oceans?

See how much you know!

How much of the Earth is covered in ocean water?

What are the names of the five oceans?

What types of food do we get from the ocean?

How do the oceans affect the weather?

What does overfishing mean?

Where is the 'Mid-Atlantic ridge'?

How do scientists study the ocean floor?

What is causing the sea levels to rise?

Key words

Coral

Algae	**Continent**
Current	**Fossil**
Mammal	**Ocean**
Pollution	**Seafood**
Seagrass	**Seaweed**
Shellfish	**Tide**
Wave	**Whale**

Glossary

Condense – To turn from a gas into a liquid.

Continent – One of the main land masses of the Earth. For example, Africa.

Equator – An imaginary line that runs around the centre of planet Earth.

Evaporate – When a liquid, such as water, turns into a gas.

Friction – When two surfaces rub together they create friction.

Generator – A machine that is used to produce electricity.

Gills – A fish's breathing organs.

Global warming – An increase in the temperature on Earth. This may be caused by a build-up of carbon dioxide in the atmosphere.

Plankton – Tiny plants and animals which live in the ocean.

Sunlit zone – The top part of the ocean.

Index